**BOOTSIE
LAURIDSEN**

Pandemic Saga: Day by Day in Couplets
Copyright © 2022 by Bootsie Lauridsen
All rights reserved. No part of this publication may be reproduced, distributed, or transmitted in any form or by any means, including photocopying, recording, or other electronic or mechanical methods, without the prior written permission of the copyright holder, except in the case of brief quotations embodied in critical reviews and certain other noncommercial uses permitted by copyright law. For permission requests, write to the publisher, addressed "Attention: Permissions Coordinator," at the address below.
ISBN Softcover: 978-1-64318-102-8
ISBN Hardcover: 978-1-64318-103-5

703 Eighth St.
Baldwin City, KS, 66006
www.imperiumpublishing.com

PANDEMIC SAGA
DAY BY DAY in COUPLETS

BOOTSIE LAURIDSEN

Baldwin City, KS

CHRONOLOGICAL
MARCH 13, 2020 — JANUARY 20, 2021

THIS BOOK IS DEDICATED TO

The millions of people who lost their lives to Covid 19.
All health care workers and vaccine scientists.
The chronological history of the Pandemic.
The reliable news outlets who wrote the facts each day.

2020 Pandemic Saga

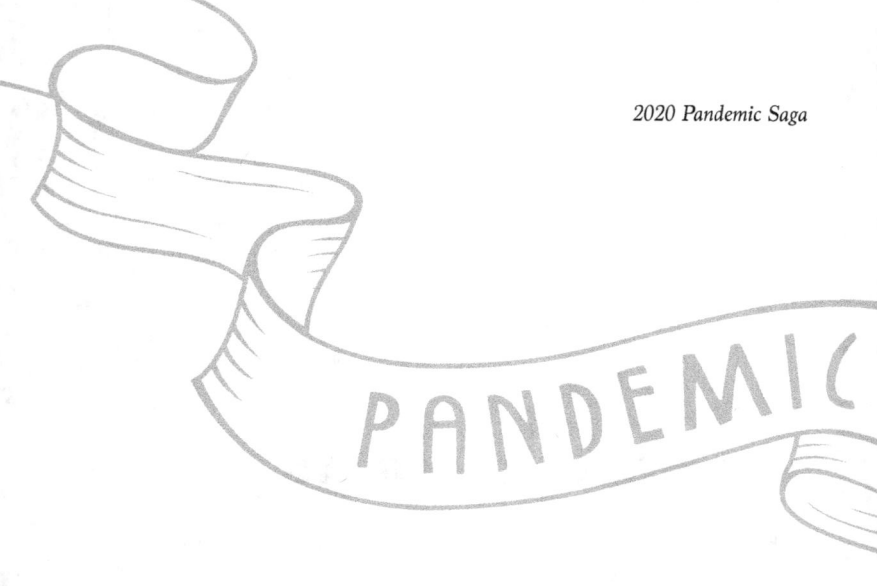

Covid-19 shut the whole world down.
Its scope virtually unknown.

Uncertainty our new certain,
Like a behind a curtain.

And then as Covid persevered,
Losing sequence of facts, I feared.

When much happened every day,
It needed order to replay.

Somehow had to keep track of time,
So I captured events in rhyme.

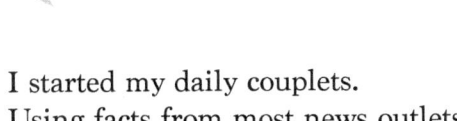

I started my daily couplets.
Using facts from most news outlets.

Our lives were changed, ready or not.
Survival mode is what we got.

One day life's normal, worries few.
Next day, chaos, what do we do?

Here's what happened, and how we coped.
Desperate ... fearful....yet we hoped.

Stock market crashed, business was dead.
Economy could not be fed.

Lost paychecks the most tragic thing.
Making workers' idle hands wring.

One day jobs here, next day they're not.
Who's going to put soup in the pot?

Forty million unemployed.
Americans bear one huge void.

Stuck at home doing odds and ends.
We called and heard from long lost friends.

Schools closed for the rest of the year.
Graduates missed what we held dear.

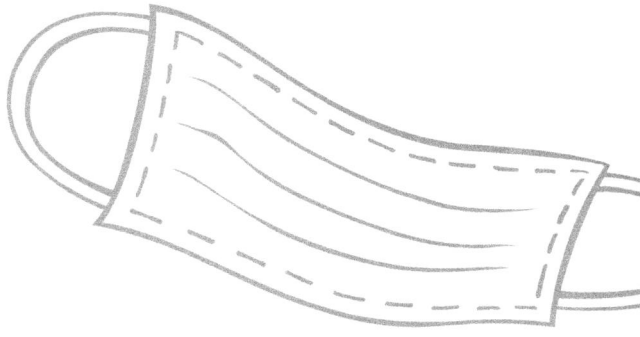

Parents became teachers each day.
They learned teachers need better pay.

We knew so little, played by ear.
Dismissed air-born droplets, no fear.

Then realized it wasn't true.
So now "wear face masks" is the cue.

Worn to keep germs from out or in.
Too bad, could be hiding a grin.

This virus seemed a distant fact,
until loved ones felt the impact.

I knew the fear it presented.
They recovered, it relented.

One thousand piece puzzles the best,
If filling up time is your quest.

Couldn't find puzzles in a store.
Everyone knew what they were for.

CNN and King of Queens.
Doomsday, laughter balanced my scenes.

Sleeping late, so lazy we got.
In scheme of things, really, why not?

No wipes, soap, or toilet paper.
Hoarding became quite a caper.

Pantries and store shelves depleted.
Grocery shopping defeated.

So many were home baking bread,
No yeast in stores, so cake instead.

Handshakes and hugs, acts of the past,
They were habits that may not last.

Sports pages, weekends were dreary.
No March Madness simply eerie.

No haircuts deemed no tragedy.
Quite soon we all looked raggedy.

Groups less than ten, six feet apart.
Social distancing not in our heart.

Max distancing on-line with Zoom.
Faces on screen in squares did loom.

Friends sent daily virus cartoons,
Brought laughter as we're all buffoons.

Honest science made Trump grouchy.
But, we believed Doctor Fauci.

Hoax is what our leader calls *it*,
To fight *it* would give *it* credit.

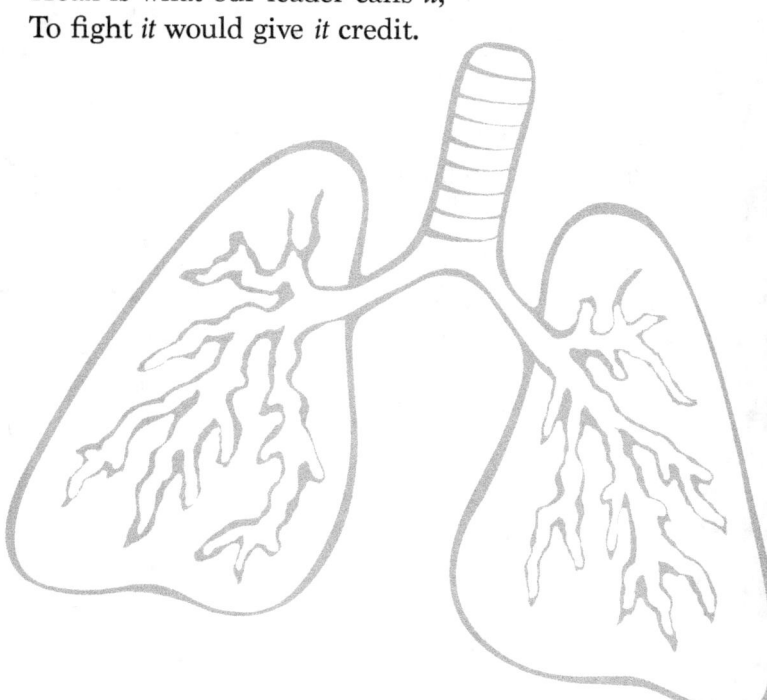

Could not ignore the politic,
When it entwined with Pandemic.

Most hospitals filled to the brim.
Stretched healthcare became pretty grim.

Docs, nurses, aides and EMTs.
Threatened their lives for you's and me's.

Equipment and protective gear,
in short supply which added fear.

States competed for these items.
No Federal help caused problems.

Nursing homes were incubators.
Window visits as closed were doors.

Mental health becomes a concern.
As despair and fear took their turn.

Playgrounds like crime scenes are red-taped.
The killer virus has escaped.

Chuck E. Cheese files for bankruptcy.
Where will kids' birthday parties be?

When a loved one took their last breath,
We couldn't meet to share their death.

Then *it* became a two-edged sword.
Health or jobs, a public discord.

A terrible dichotomy.
Infection against poverty.

Economy must re-instate.
So our country can operate.

Three months of isolation,
Seems a human violation.

Testing and tracing were the keys,
Too few on hand for allottees.

Testing to see if you've got *it*.
Tracing to see who you visit.

Reason it's hard to terminate,
Takes fourteen days to incubate.

Might be fourteen days symptom free.
Yet give that bug to somebody.

Re-starting has to be done right.
Shut down again, an ugly sight.

Every state opened its own way.
Total confusion was the day.

Help from the top would have been great.
Guidelines could have helped every state.

No Presidential leadership.
Re-entry was a bumpy trip.

Workers wary of re-entry.
Torn between need and jeopardy.

Restaurants were among first starts.
Laid-off workers had grateful hearts.

But masks, great for not spreading *stuff*.
Made eating and drinking real tough.

Trump touts Hydroxychloroquine,
Not a vaccine and unproven.

Trump opened all churches today.
So now we can worship and pray.

But we found out worship and prayer,
Can be done safely anywhere.

Memorial Day we took the plunge.
Soaked up gathering like a sponge.

Here is the data for USA.
On this grim Memorial Day:
1,644,143 Infected
97,724 Deaths

Then Racism worries did spike.
When policeman's bad choice did strike.

Sat with his knee on George Floyd's neck.
Nine minutes with never a check.

"I can't breathe" his desperate cries.
We saw him die before our eyes.

Cell phones caught this repugnant act.
George Floyd was murdered, that's the fact.

Black people are living in dread.
Black safety just held by a thread.

Many marched in peaceful protest.
Rioters came to cause unrest.

We wait again for fourteen days.
To see if surge makes its displays.

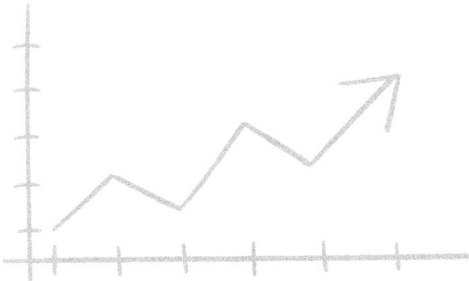

We now have three epidemics,
Viral, Racial, Economics.

As end of "stay at home" abates,
Cases rising in half the states.

Opening up too soon was feared.
We did! Guess what? The spikes appeared.

Texas re-opened as the first.
Spike in patients sadly the worst.

Europe has banned Americans,
As we don't take safe precautions.

And, Trump is waiting for the day,
Covid will simply "go away."

New social media called Twitch.
Gave Trump another verbal itch.

Not for long, Twitch closed his account.
Hateful themes were hard to discount.

Trump plans rallies amidst the fears.
Because he badly needs the cheers.

To attend must sign to abstain,
From suing the grand Trump campaign.

June jobs outlook is sobering,
As layoffs are still occurring.

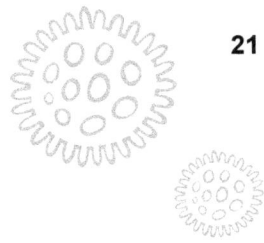

Now we're open, no restrictions,
Boldly snubbing all predictions.

Throwing ourselves under the bus.
The virus is not through with us.

Virus surging in half the states.
Will soon be over, Trump debates.

Spiking not hypothetical.
Next two weeks will be critical.

Here's the data for USA
Day after Happy Fathers' Day.
2,377,268 Infected
22,528 Deaths

MLB back end of July.
No one in stands to see balls fly.

Don't need fans to watch on TV.
Will be a bit of normalcy.

States make plans to re-open schools.
When, what, how, need consistent rules.

Curve on the rise for 40 states.
Single worse day since early dates.

No fans there for Nascar Races.
So what? Drivers can't see faces.

End of June, bills still piled.
42 mil. jobless claims filed.

Here is the data for USA
on the July Fourth holiday.
3,445,500 Infections
136,356 Deaths

Numbers reveal the human loss.
But lives are changed in the chaos.

Americans need more patience.
It's not our greatest forbearance.

Trump's not against covering his face.
But says masks have a time and place.

Businesses want nightmare to end.
New nightmare just around the bend.

Trump gave orders to open the schools,
But, not his place to set the rules.

Now know droplets a dire affair.
Last longer, go farther in air.

White House blasts Fauci's honesty,
For slowing the recovery.

No one's paid any attention.
Solution is the prevention!

Moderna's vaccine tests look great.
To find it safe will be long wait.

And now we face with much chagrin,
That we could get Covid again.

Aftermath might also contain,
Conditions of heart, skin and brain.

Survivor Corps, a Facebook pool,
Great therapy and research tool.

Athletes are gathering to prepare,
And getting infected while there.

Seems peaks compete to up the score.
Each peak higher than one before.

The mask mandates an idle threat.
No bad penalties as of yet.

July brought hefty fines to pay.
"Mask up or pay up," in L.A.

Coming elections took back seat.
Candidates can't meet or greet.

Dems. will have online convention.
Reps. going live, damn prevention.

Russia hacked our vaccine info.
Next our election? We'll never know.

Antibodies role, elusive,
as test results, inconclusive.

Whether they prevent and protect,
Nobody knows what to expect.

UK vaccine seems to work.
China's too, but danger could lurk.

Alarming new highs and death tolls.
At mid-July, this virus rolls.

Curve, surge, and peak, words used each week.
Never hear low numbers we seek.

Trump brought his daily briefings back.
Staff wonders if he'll stay on track.

Baseball season started this week.
Piped in crowd noise, like tongue in cheek.

Cardboard cut-outs in stands too much.
Tom Hanks, popcorn vendor, nice touch.

But, on TV it seems the same.
Still a great way to watch a game.

1.4 mil. seek jobless aid.
Congress can't deem if they'll be paid.

Job aid stops at end of July.
Still no jobs to help them get by.

Senate thinks aid acts like a perk,
So they fear jobless won't seek work.

Opening schools up in the air.
Not much time for all to prepare.

School boards deciding year's design.
School or combined with home online.

They're facing the same old question.
Back to work or less infection.

Trump canceled his grand convention.
Never before sought prevention.

Now both conventions scaled back.
Working hard to plan their attack.

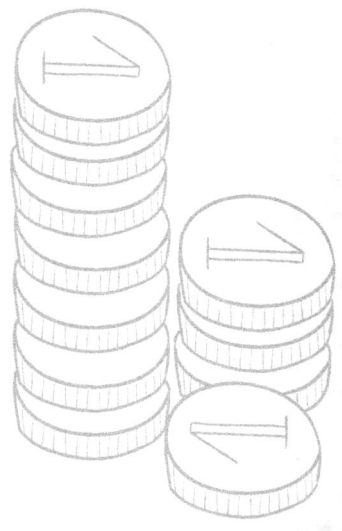

Deaths in Kansas keep on rising.
Not wearing masks, not surprising.

Coins are now Pandemic shortage.
Staying at home reduced their flowage.

Fragments of Covid shed in stool.
Testing sewage is tracing tool.

Coke makers couldn't meet demands.
So stopped making the lesser brands.

Humans start testing the vaccines.
Yet to learn what the testing gleans.

Long term testing is what we need,
To make a safe vaccine, indeed.

Virus must like heat and sweat.
Eighteen Marlin players have *it.*

As more Trump's advisers get sick.
"Not been around them," is his shtick.

Pro sports teams determined to play.
NBA season starts today.

To avoid the Covid trouble,
Teams played their games in a "bubble".

Conspiracy theories alive,
On social media beehive.

Congress left for weekend, no deal.
If their pay stopped, how would they feel?

Fearing Covid, mailed ballots sent.
Trump says they could be fraudulent.

Here's the data for USA
For the end of July
4,405,932 Infections
150,000 Deaths

July marks most cases since March.
The highest peak on its arch.

All our hearts ask when will this end?
Our minds say not around the bend.

Covid challenges hurricane.
Florida stops test sites for rain.

Will be no election delay,
But late results will bring dismay.

Primary polls' safety ensured.
Mailed ballots will be secured.

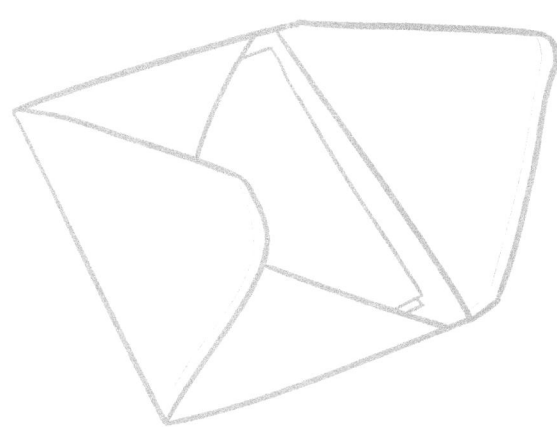

While virus news seems more of same,
Summer Covid spreads like a flame.

Parents fret as schools may open,
Not knowing just what will happen.

Balancing jobs and home schooling.
Their situation is confusing.

Teachers, too, are left in the lurch.
On precarious wires they perch.

Trumps mandates opening schools.
The virus wins and calls us fools.

Headlines not about Pandemic,
But plights it brought to the public.

September most schools are opening.
To everyone this is frightening.

Teachers named essential workers.
Will fight the virus like soldiers.

Opening schools good for the heart.
Keeping them open the hard part.

Last-ditch virus aid talks collapsed.
Relief for millions has relapsed.

Executive orders Trump used.
for not being legal, he's accused.

With many food industries closed,
Bare grocery shelves again exposed.

With the cost of food out of sight.
No pay checks added to the plight.

Dozens state health officials leave,
As science many don't believe.

Trump gives aid for unemployment.
Wants strapped states to help with payment.

Most deaths in USA since May.
The curve not heading the right way.

Russia registers first vaccine.
Safety elements are foreseen.

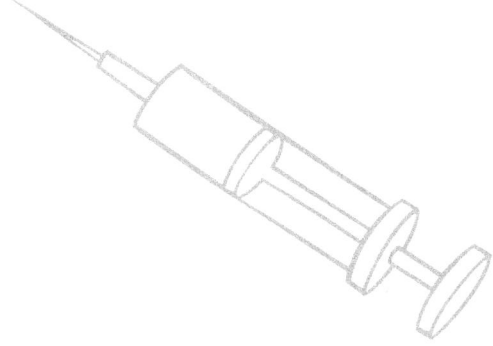

Rise in jobless claims in headlines,
As workplace struggles with declines.

NCAA warning college sports.
Start now and your season aborts.

Test method, saliva direct.
NBA testing its effect.

Covid deaths fall, new cases rise,
Which seems to be a real surprise.

Democrats call postal hearing.
Damage done, election nearing.

Unconventional conventions.
Dems first to tell their convictions.

"We the people." Dems. new slogan.
It's constitution's main notion.

August sixth month, Covid still here.
Opening schools comes with much fear.

Colleges, schools are now hot spots.
They open, they close, Covid trots.

Trump says he's blocking P.O. cash.
To make mail-in votes cause backlash.

Says they will halt what they've begun.
But not undo what they have done.

Garages, driveways, new parlors,
As gatherings safer outdoors.

In Kansas, cases rebounding.
Just when schools are re-opening.

Almost half will attend in-school.
But plans change daily, is the rule.

Economy getting better,
As ads make newspapers thicker.

Covid plasma okay to give,
Covid patients a chance to live.

Republican Convention starts.
Virtually and not, it imparts.

Vaccine sharing will bring complaints.
Supply and need require restraints.

Distribution requires thought,
Because it will be worldwide sought.

Covid not waning in our state,
With sixth highest infection rate.

Jobless claims high, layoffs persist.
Hard to get jobs that don't exist.

Most schools opening next week.
Health problems teachers didn't seek.

Each district's doing it's own thing.
No consistency does it bring.

Some grades half in-school, half out.
Some staggered days in weeks throughout.

Man first to get Covid twice here,
With Covid symptoms more severe.

Why aren't we doing all we can,
To keep elections safe again?

Kenosha showed Racism's smack.
Seven shots in a black man's back.

NBA's, Doc Rivers, did say,
After shooting that dreadful day.

"Amazed why we love our country,
When our country doesn't love us back."

College towns experiencing spikes,
Social gatherings and the likes.

On-line course from home, an ordeal.
On-line course from dorm, more appeal.

Here's the Data for USA
On August's last day
6,032,100 Infections
183,279 Deaths

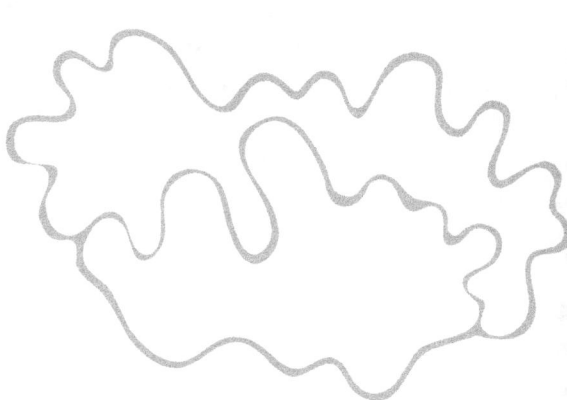

Eviction rates soar in Kansas.
Need extended help from Congress.

CDC says vaccine here shortly.
Asks states to make plans directly.

Rich states have bargained for vaccine.
Poor states will find their supply lean.

U.S. Covid cases decline.
To June levels, today's headline.

Evictions now banned for a year.
Renters are protected from fear.

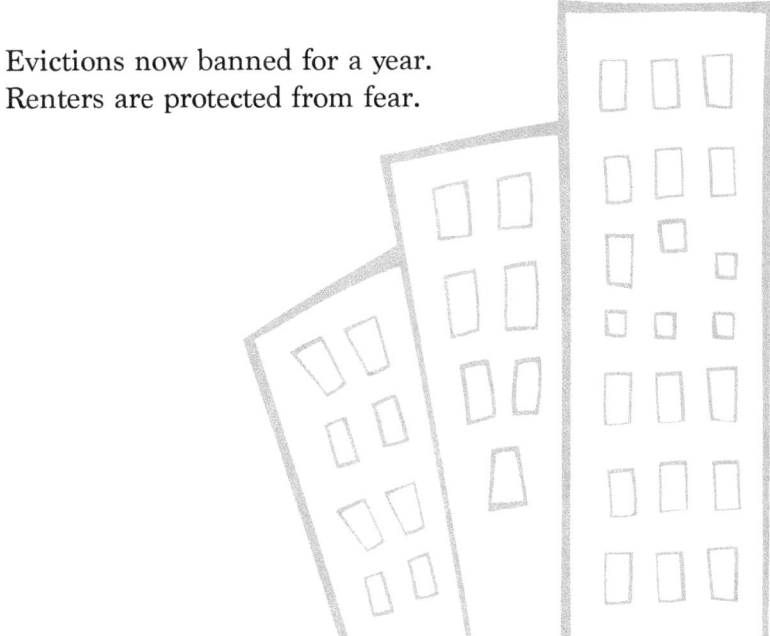

"The year of our fragility,"
Leonard Pitts' quotability.

Graveside services have replaced,
Funerals where you can't be spaced.

Trump said, vote by mail, then at poll.
Questioning returns is his goal.

Steroids help Covid patients live.
Studies show the "whys" elusive.

Right now country's holding its breath.
Hoping Labor Day won't bring death.

For mental health, most could agree.
Life would be worse without TV.

Today is start of most all schools,
With hope, care, and new learning tools.

Masks, temp checks are new this school year.
ALL is new for virtual sphere.

GOP rolls out relief bill.
Dems don't like, so stalled on the hill.

Final stage vaccine trial whopped.
Person in test ill, trial stopped.

Bob Woodard tapes prove that Trump knew.
That Covid was more than the flu.

On tape, "Deadly stuff," what Trump said,
But to us played it down instead.

Said he wanted to stop panic.
So hide the truth, where's the ethic?

Needed those facts to keep us well
Now we've had seven months of Hell.

As need for jobless relief grows,
Means market recovery slows.

Now daily Covid news is slight.
Though cases rise, and still a fright.

We're numb from all the virus strife.
Seeing it's our new way of life.

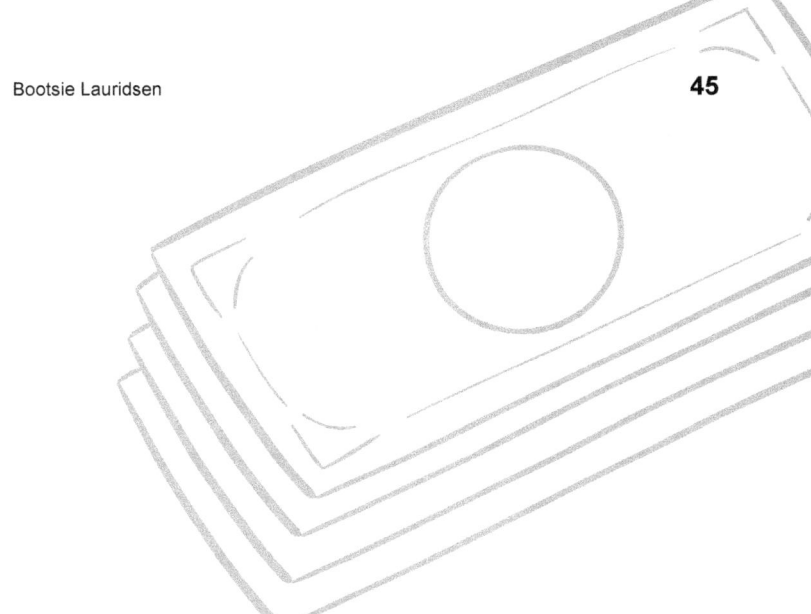

Distance mandates hard to enforce.
Public consent, only recourse.

Unemployed struggle to survive.
New relief aid, yet to arrive.

Pelosi keeps house in session,
Till relief rescue concession.

Trump wants bigger relief bill penned.
Wants cash in people's hands to spend.

Democrats embraced his demands.
Now is in the GOP's hands.

Europe shuns lock downs in wave two.
Going to hot spots to subdue.

CDC relaxed when to test,
Then reversed back to what seemed best.

So it's hard to know what is right.
Even experts find truth a plight.

Phone app can namelessly tell us.
If we're around one with virus.

Would be helpful tracing device.
But, state health info imprecise.

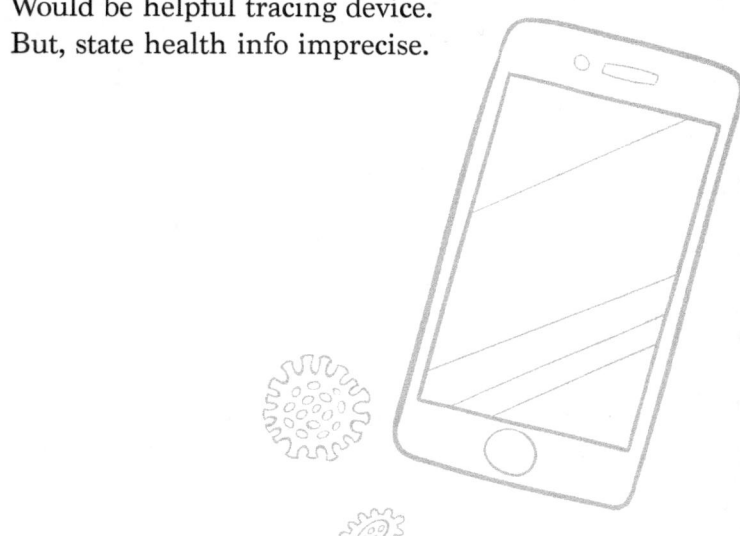

CDC said droplets fall fast.
Then said in air they seem to last.

Justice Ruth Bader Ginsburg died.
Trying to live, the court to guide.

Another sad national blow.
Getting tough to go with the flow.

Now the fight for her replacement.
Trump says "NOW" and will implement.

More Kansas schools going remote.
And, likewise, can't keep sports afloat.

Virtual schooling hard on moms.
Retail jobs present mom problems.

Shifts vary widely week to week,
So, have to quit, not choice they seek.

Plaza Art Show adjusts to plight.
Puts art in store fronts in plain sight.

Dems to redraft virus relief.
Must try again is their belief.

New Covid cases raise concerns.
Peaked mid-July, now surge returns.

Trump wants vaccine out right away.
Says tight restrictions cause delay.

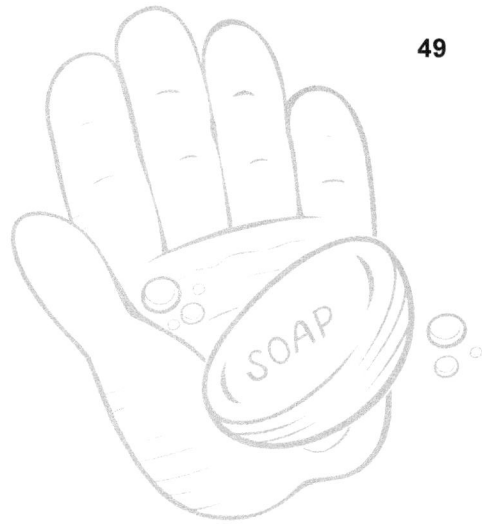

Kansas hits new high for cases.
Starting schools are not safe places.

Global death toll passes three mil.
Makes you ask, is there an "until?"

These aren't just numbers, they're humans.
Mothers, fathers, daughters, and sons.

Here's the data for USA
On September's last day:
7,434,572 Infections
211,464 Deaths

Due to much hand washing and more.
Paper towels gone from the store.

Flu vaccine advised to prevent.
A "Twindemic", a Fall event.

This year just got more disruptive.
Trump and wife have tested positive.

This has great ramifications,
The gravest of situations.

Sent to Walter Reed for good care.
Walked to copter, thumb up in air.

Two NFL games moved today.
Too many "positives" to play.

Little news on Trump's condition.
We'll know when cleared by physician.

While still sick, Trump made reckless plans.
He took a ride to wave at fans.

Job gains slow as layoffs persist.
Makes it hard for folks to exist.

Regal's movie screens go dark.
Fighting Covid was hopeless lark.

Trump left hospital today.
These were the words he sent our way.

"Don't fear Covid," and took off mask.
"How cavalier is that," we ask?

Marched with staff to Oval Office,
Exposing staff to his virus.

White House now a "no mask zone."
Thirty-six cases have been sown.

Positive White House staff not seen.
Country's managed from quarantine.

Trump stops talks on relief action.
Then tweets, "Till I win election."

Most Kansas counties in red zone.
In-school classes should not open.

Next debate will be virtual.
Trump won't do it, they'll have control.

Trump calls his drug cocktail his cure.
But, won't test to see if that's sure.

Stocks jumped on stimulus hopes.
But, for now they're dead on the ropes.

"Herd Immunity" now a goal.
Odd way of thinking as a whole.

Pandemic slammed small business,
Not good for economy's mess.

Jobless claims now at record highs,
While lay-offs continue to rise.

Infections hit Harris campaign,
So in person events not sane.

P.O. reversed its cuts in June.
Seems too late to be opportune.

Trump's put fear in voting process.
Saying we'll see potential mess.

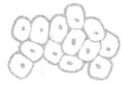

Election heads make it clear.
All voting is safe as ever.

Vaccine's urgency causes fears.
Insuring its safety takes years.

"Covid fatigue" new descriptive,
Making us much less restrictive.

Having this funk makes us careless,
Yearning for life before madness.

Rapid tests now available.
But, results are untraceable.

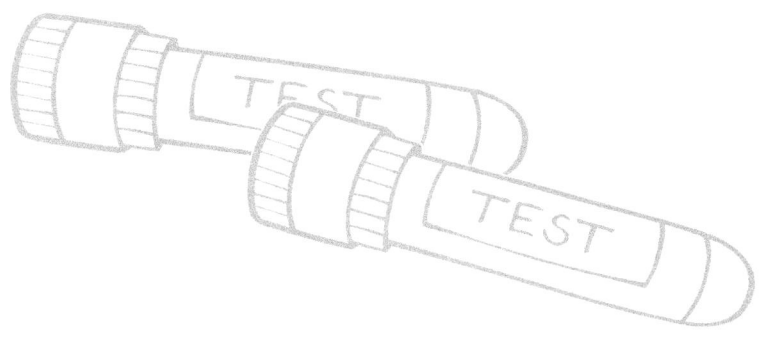

At-home tests, FDA okayed.
Only those with symptoms got aid.

This third wave caught sister and mate.
In fatigue, they did vegetate.

Both had never felt so distressed.
After 10 days, ate and got dressed.

Stopped vaccine studies restarting.
FDA won't allow rushing.

Highest new case numbers yet.
Hospitals in crisis, they fret.

Covid and election fatigue,
Make mental health hard to achieve.

Covid's threatening Thanksgivings.
Gut wrenching decisions it brings.

Europe tried shortened quarantine.
Now have lockdowns, a dreaded scene.

States must get ready for vaccine.
So far, no guidelines have been seen.

Here's the data for USA
On this Halloween Day
9,377,348 Infections
235,810 Deaths

Halloween questions trick or treats.
Little carriers walk the streets.

Now have rapid response testing.
National strategy missing.

Presidential election race,
Sanity or "in your face."

Safety at the polls is troubling.
New record set for early voting.

Store fronts boarded-up in cities,
Fearing protest activities.

Covid virus tackled my Grandson.
Only light symptoms, so he won.

Three generations kin got sick.
We need to have vaccine and quick.

Covid does not discriminate.
Wrong place, wrong time could be our fate.

Election Day finally here.
No one knows who will persevere.

The day after election day,
White House race is too close to say.

Trump says "quit counting," courts say "no."
This proves process is law, courts say so.

But, Covid wins in USA,
As new case record set today.

Third day still counting in five states.
Razor thin leads, winner awaits.

Fifth day out, Biden is winner.
Vote margin couldn't be thinner.

Change came, Biden new President.
His job tough, problems evident.

Pandemic's his priority.
To help health and economy.

If he can is a mystery,
But will become his history.

Still feeling election fatigue,
As Trump simply will not concede.

Our country's sharply divided.
Each thinks, the other's misguided.

This third wave is causing trouble,
Breaks the "feeling safer" bubble.

Trump and staff won't help transition.
Puts country in bad position.

Pfizer's vaccine has been approved.
Much of our fear may be removed.

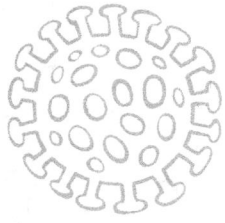

Every day Covid's records fall.
Threatens hospitals, schools, et al.

U.S. ramps for vaccination,
Biggest effort in the nation.

News-- masks also protect wearers.
Double reason to be bearers.

Japanese tests on mannequins,
Proved masks kept spray from out and ins.

Virus at most dangerous stage,
And Trump won't try to turn the page.

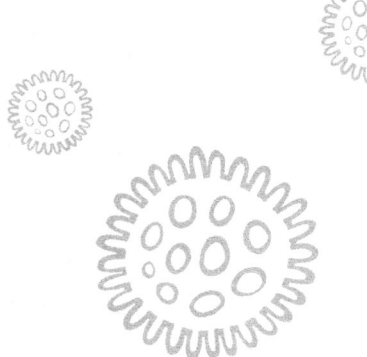
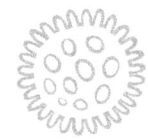

Biden, hindered, does what he can,
Gathers experts, data, and plans.

A second vaccine appears good.
It was under Moderna's hood.

Distribution is next big test,
Needs federal guidelines at best.

Rapid self-testing kits here for use.
How to get them now is abstruse.

Still no Covid relief for states,
While "no jobs" crisis impacts fates.

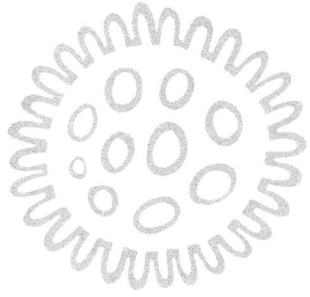  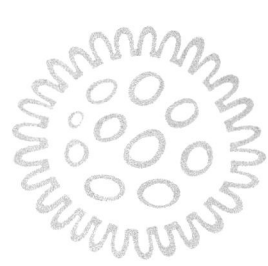

Unseen symptom, anxiety.
Hovering in reality.

Holidays, sadly, won't be great.
Old traditions will have to wait.

Third vaccine--Oxford's--protects more,
And no difficult temps to store.

NYC schools close again.
Ways to fight Covid getting thin.

Hospitals are overflowing.
Overwhelmed staffs are despairing.

Take note this virus is airborne.
Scrubbing surfaces overdrawn.

Forty-seven states in Red Zone.
We can't believe it's overblown.

Countless Covid corpses in morgues.
National Guard helped with the hordes.

Big turkeys were not bought this year.
Turkey raisers living their fear.

Stores brace as viral enemy,
Bears down on our economy.

GSA approved transition,
So no longer Trump's decision.

Antibody drug cleared, they tell,
To help high risk patients get well.

Many questions follow the vaccine.
Who, how, when? Answers not foreseen.

Oxford medicine results, troubling.
Pfizer, Moderna, less guessing.

CDC panel will soon say,
Where vaccine's priorities lay.

Then states have to make their plans.
Distribution is in their hands.

Jobless claims rise second straight week,
Making economy's health bleak.

North Dakota's numbers unfurled,
Highest Covid rates in the world.

New York's church attendance not blocked.
High court ruling, Pandemic mocked.

States taking up Covid funding,
As federal money not forthcoming.

Trump shouts election plot theories,
Causing fearful unrest worries.

Here's the data for USA
On November's last day.
13,766,662 Infections
273,302 Deaths

"Pandemic" chosen word of the Year.
A daily word we see and hear.

Congress back for aid endeavor,
More important now than ever.

Moderna asks for vaccine use,
As Pfizer did in last week's news.

Pfizer vaccine cleared for UK,
For emergency use, they say.

Going to most vulnerable,
Nursing homes/staffs are in trouble.

The approved, is two-dose vaccine,
Could cause some problems yet unseen.

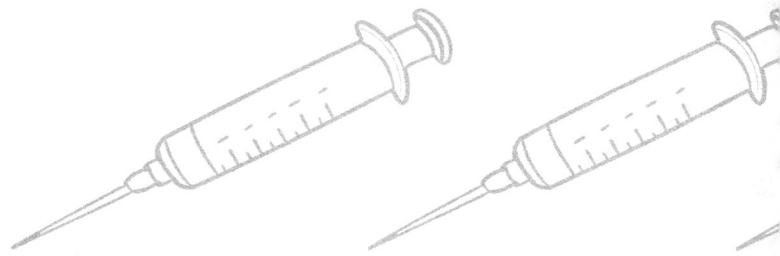

Three vaccines wait for our OK:
Pfizer, Moderna, J & J.

Pfizer, Moderna are two shot.
But Johnson & Johnson is not.

Vaccines build our immune system,
To fight cases, not prevent them.

Pfizer needs low sub zero temp.
Other two, low temp exempt.

Denmark killed fourteen million mink,
To stop a strain with Covid link.

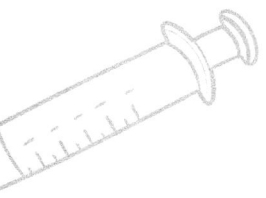

Some schools are closing till April.
Parents and teachers will grumble.

Serve your country, Biden will ask.
For one hundred days, wear a mask.

Some places shorten quarantines.
Bad timing is what that means.

Some fear vaccines aren't safe to take.
Rushed process speed does caution make.

Covid's now country's top killer.
The vaccine will be our pillar.

The cost for vaccine will be free.
But for service, might be a fee.

Each state's planning distribution.
Which is causing much confusion.

We need national strategies,
To prevent needless tragedies.

First vaccine shot in West given,
To woman, 90, in Britain.

FDA gives final okay.
Pfizer vaccine is on the way.

None too soon, death records shattered.
Life as we knew it is tattered.

Biggest vaccination effort.
Now it needs everyone's support.

It also gives a dose of hope,
Ending Pandemic is its scope.

Will only work if it's taken.
If we don't, cause forsaken.

Vaccine brings some complications,
Temp, shipping, handling, locations.

UPS and Fed Ex helping.
Cold vaccine boxes they're shipping.

With GPS sensors to check,
Temps and locations on their trek.

Walmart, Walgreens, and CVS,
Partners to help with the process.

First shots delivered tomorrow,
To health staffs, nursing homes also.

Vaccine serum went to all states.
Shots for phase one out of the gates.

Not even enough for phase one.
Hope distribution is well-run.

Specifics of future phases,
Unclear and questions it raises.

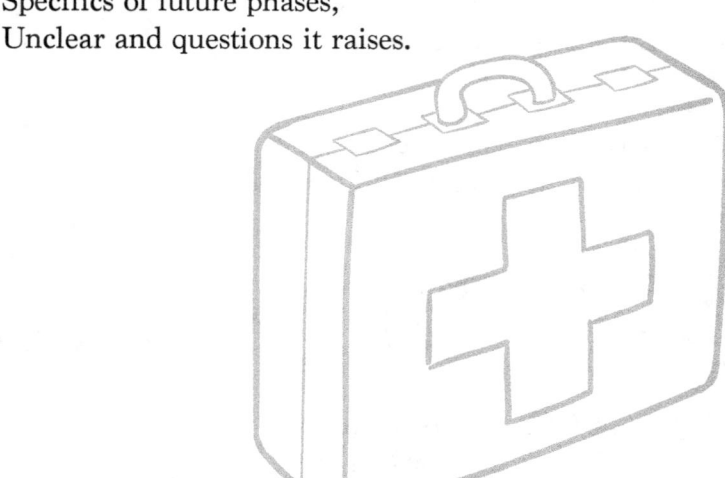

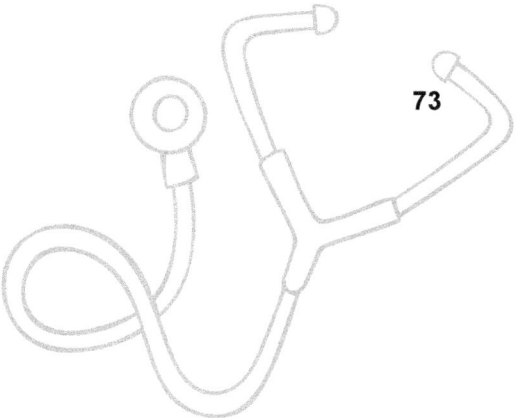

First shots to New York doc and nurse.
While in the midst of Covid's curse.

Electors confirm Biden's win.
Democracy at work again.

Hospitals, ICUs maxed out,
Medical crisis, there's no doubt.

Morgues as well, and for help they asked.
Fatality care, a huge task.

Kansas receives vaccine at last.
Shipment much lower than forecast.

Unemployment claims most ever.
Help must come now, not later.

At-home Covid test is approved.
Rapid results, red tape removed.

Vaccine shots now at nursing homes,
Where Covid so easily roams.

Teachers get vaccine in phase two,
And more at-risk people thereto.

General public in phase three.
Not for many months will it be.

In these times, masks still critical,
Science based, not political.

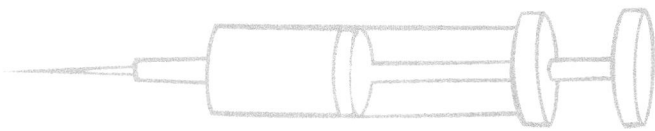

Don't know what safety vaccines give.
Yet with unknowns, can't be passive.

Moderna's vaccine cleared, we read.
Will help us have vaccine we need.

Congress set virus aid amount,
Six hundred dollars at last count.

Vaccine and testing scams are here.
Gave crooks a chance to con this year.

Christmas had unexpected gift.
New Covid strain has gone adrift.

This new virus strain plagues Britain.
World is tense as will be smitten.

Doctors changing Covid treatment,
Respirators, last deferment.

Millions of Denmark's killed mink,
Now rotting and causing big stink.

They were buried, but their gasses,
Exposed them to air in masses.

In Kansas, virus still raging.
Half the state, masks not engaging.

Colder weather drives us inside.
Where safety measures are denied.

Things overlooked for prevention,
Ventilation and filtration.

Trump says he may not sign aid bill.
A lot of Christmas hope would kill.

Mad at GOP, he disses,
For not following his wishes.

U.S. just ordered more vaccine.
One hundred mil shots to our scene.

Data points to immunity,
After infection certainty.

Rare for it to happen again.
Only time will tell if certain.

Autopsies key to fight Covid.
Information gained not morbid.

Explains the wide range of symptoms,
Giving treatment fewer problems.

Lives are saved by looking at death,
Giving knowledge much deeper breadth.

Found new strain is more contagious.
They don't know why so infectious.

No signs this strain is more severe,
And Fauci says it's surely here.

Pfizer assures that their vaccine,
Should protect us from the new strain.

Key is high vaccination rate.
That should help Pandemic abate.

Some states impose stricter lockdowns,
As Covid rises in their towns.

P.O. sabotaged earlier.
Cuts made their job more severe.

DeJoy said they would not cut more.
But, what was cut, did not restore.

P.O. swamped by Christmas event.
More than normal gifts, cards were sent.

Cards and packages still on the go.
Sent three weeks ago, more than slow.

Covid surges and restraints fall.
Families win and airports full.

Relief aid is stalled as Trump rants,
As do all the recipients.

House passed 600 buck bill.
Then a mess on Capitol Hill.

Trump signed this bill after old one lapsed.
Next day, for $2,000, he asked?

Trump uses political clout,
And this is what it's all about.

Then House voted for this amount.
Now to Senate for final count.

McConnell blocks vote to boost aid.
Making needy wait to be paid.

Meanwhile, aid benefits are lost.
At a huge, tragic, human cost.

More people want to take vaccine,
Where resistance was earlier seen.

Distribution still a struggle.
State plans have encountered trouble.

Kansas distribution, a mess,
Hindered by a red-tape process.

Plus, too few doses for phase one.
Even health workers not all done.

No tracking of distribution,
Gives no info on transmission.

General public in the dark.
We don't know how things will embark.

We don't know who, how, when or where.
Knowing a plan would clear the air.

LA hospitals more than full.
Ambulance turned away, dreadful.

Now case of new strain in CO.
Highly contagious, that we know.

Our cases down in South and West.
Christmas, New Year will be the test.

Now viral strain found in CA.
Seems this new strain is on its way.

Oxford-Astra-Zeneca used,
In UK as strain was exposed.

That vaccine's cheap, easy to store.
None held back, so they could reach more.

This one-shot method set for fate.
World's new way to inoculate.

Six hundred dollar checks are paid,
As McConnell backs Congress aid.

Time Square a ghost town New Year's Eve.
Ball drop seen only on T.V.

Deadliest month is December,
Of worst year we can remember.

Here's the data for USA
On December's last day.
83,489,065 Infected
1,819,913 Deaths

Pandemic is not through with us.
History goes on despite our fuss.

Virus is raging uncontrolled.
Covid tsunami, we are told.

Kansas has an unwanted fate,
The lowest national shot rate.

UK gives shots for all in need.
Shorting dose for next shot, indeed.

Giving first shots to all is done.
Thinks one shot is better than none.

Dr Fauci, "Not doing that."
We need to follow dose format.

Plenty of vaccine is on hand.
Distribution has not been grand.

With no plans, dilemma for states,
Haste and ignorance on their plates.

Vandals target congress leaders.
Spray painted their homes with angers.

Kansas to use genetic test,
To help with new Covid's strain quest.

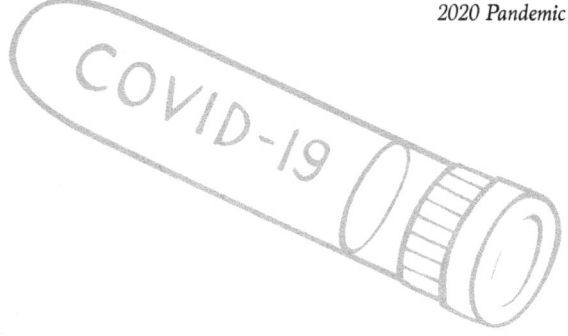

As new strains spread very quickly,
Vaccinations must come swiftly.

Still don't know when I can get shot,
Or if I'm in phase one or not.

First given shots in USA,
Got their second shot yesterday.

As many shots not delivered,
Thoughts of dose sharing considered.

Scotland mandates stay home order.
So has England on their border.

Variants are new versions sowed,
In a virus genetic code.

Covid wins race around the world.
Distribution problems unfurled.

Record deaths are daily posted.
Long way from this virus busted.

Trump's fans stormed Capitol Building,
Urged by him to do his bidding.

Halting the job proving his loss.
They then faced frightening chaos.

Some lawmakers squeezed in shelter,
Tested positive days later.

After twelve hours fearfully spun,
They went back to work, got it done.

That day showed Trump's dangerous flaws,
And why Covid was not his cause.

State vaccine rollout hindered.
No support or money rendered.

State's public health is on its own.
Budgets had been cut to the bone.

Biden's talking to state leaders,
About distribution matters.

Specifics how to get it done,
Federal help where there's been none.

Pfizer's vaccine's second shots due.
This a vaccine saved for first few.

Biden wants to use all vaccine
For first shots to all as a screen.

He'll lever private industry,
To meet second shots handily.

Cases, hospital care, deaths rise.
When will Pandemic stabilize?

Now trying mass vaccination.
Long waits not an attraction.

Big venue parking lots, the scene,
Where thousands can get the vaccine.

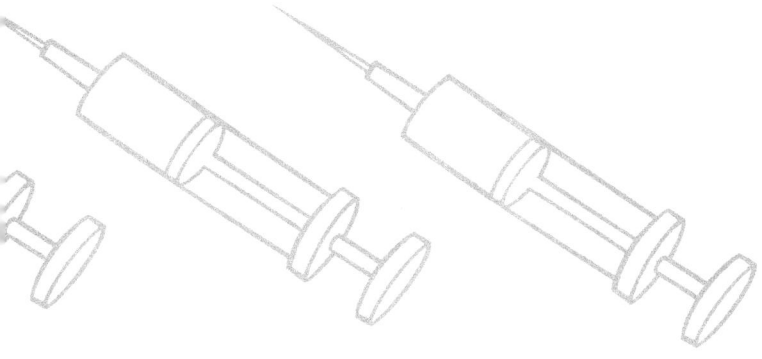

Vaccine just waiting brings alarms.
States told to get it into arms.

After House members had their say,
Trump impeached second time today.

Pandemic's deadliest day yet.
Why lowered restrictions we get?

Country wants to get back to work,
Even when infections still lurk.

Split country is in a dire dance.
Let's be sure Biden gets his chance.

WHO studies Covid's source.
Science says bats are likely force.

Team will go to Wuhan, China.
First case was from that area.

Some think it began in lab there.
Just rumor, but hangs in the air.

How safe will we be after shot?
Can we transmit Covid or not?

Due to our Capitol's attack,
Pandemic news is very slack.

Second shot doses scarce that's true.
Supply has become an issue.

All health workers are still not done.
And they are the first in Phase one.

Pfizer can't keep up with demand.
Need much more than they have on hand.

Biden gives 100 day "asks."
Hundred mil, shots, and wear masks.

A vaccination plan he'll make,
To get it done, so much at stake.

Biden's planned a Covid package,
To help recovery, his pledge.

One point nine trill. to make it work.
Some legislators that will irk.

Fragile vaccine's allocation,
To rural sites slows dispersion.

Covid strains much more contagious.
To not take care is egregious.

Covid is raging in thirty states.
Pandemic still lies on our plates.

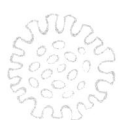

Found complications in children.
Unusual symptoms, hidden.

Global death toll does not reflect,
All deaths caused by Covid's effect.

Covid surges spur mutations,
Which threaten vaccine protections.

We know little in this short time.
Hard to know solutions to prime.

Mishandling worst public health fact.
Brought more deaths from failure to act.

Trump denied it, dumped it on states.
With no guidance to help their fates.

Today Democracy prevailed.
Biden's inauguration hailed.

Due to violence at Capitol,
Inauguration not normal.

Grounds guarded by military,
Frightfully extraordinary.

Otherwise a grand transition.
To hear Biden's plan of action.

Unity is his major plan.
If it can be done, he's the man.

Best act was Amanda Gorman
Reciting her poem, "The Hill We Climb."
Last two lines:
The new dawn blooms as we free it,
For there is always a light,
If only we're brave enough to see it.
If only we're brave enough to be it.

Here's the data for USA
On January 20, Inauguration Day
24,323,846 Infections
404,689 deaths

Ten months later, Covid prevails,
And I'm ending these epic tales.

EPILOGUE

What happened and when, a daily look.
Quick fun read, faster than a book.

Seems we're never going to be free,
To live our lives so carelessly.

Millions of lives lost in the world.
A deadly curve ball, nature hurled.

Hard decision, when to end this.
The end's unknown for this virus.

This history's been done by me,
As my Pandemic therapy.

...and Covid's saga continues.

MUCH THANKS TO:

REAL (not fake) NEWS OUTLETS: PBS News Hour, NBC, ABC, CBS, CNN, MSNBC, *Kansas City Star, Lawrence Journal World, Wall Street Journal*

Kent Lauridsen, Encouragement, Editing
Diane McQuerry, Editing
Laura Lauridsen, Editing

www.ingramcontent.com/pod-product-compliance
Lightning Source LLC
Chambersburg PA
CBHW071251070526
44583CB00017B/2427